What's in this book

This book belongs to

_____

第一次露营
Camping for the first time

学习内容 Contents

沟通 Communication

说说日常活动
Talk about your daily routine

背景介绍：
浩浩和小伙伴们第一次去露营，他们在小河边钓鱼、欣赏大自然。

生词 New words

★ 起床	to get up
★ 洗脸	to wash one's face
★ 刷牙	to brush one's teeth
★ 洗澡	to shower, to bath
★ 想	to want to, to think
★ 穿	to wear
★ 上衣	tops
★ 了	(to indicate a change of state or the completion of an action)
都	both, all
戴	to wear on top
条	(measure word for dresses, skirts, pants, etc.)

件　　　　(measure word for tops)
裙子　　dress, skirt

中国儿童的衣服
Clothes worn by Chinese children

句式 Sentence patterns

别的用品都不见了。
The other items are all missing.

你们长大了。
You have grown up.

跨学科学习 Project

制作纸帽子
Fold a paper hat

参考答案：
1 Yes, they are fishing, building a camp fire and playing hide-and-seek.
2 Yes, I believe I can./No, I do not think so.
3 I think they can because they have practised at home how to take care
of themselves when camping./I think some can and others cannot.

Get ready

1 Can you name three fun camping activities?

2 Can you take care of yourself when camping?

3 Do you think Hao Hao and his friends can take care of themselves when camping?

读一读 Read

故事大意：
浩浩和小伙伴们第一次去露营，大家都很兴奋；但是在独立生活时，他们还不能完全照顾自己。老师鼓励他们自己的事要学习自己做。

第一次一起去露营，同学们都很高兴。

参考问题和答案：

1 Do you think the children all look happy? (Yes, they all do.)

2 Which camping activities do you like most? Why? (I like the barbecue most because the marshmellows taste so good./I like singing around the camp fire the most.)

4

qǐ chuáng
起床

xǐ liǎn
洗脸

shuā yá
刷牙

早上起床后，大家开始洗脸刷牙。

参考问题和答案：

1 What is Ivan doing? (He is getting up.)
2 What is Hao Hao doing? (He is washing his face.)
3 What is the boy in pink doing? (He is brushing his teeth.)
4 Can the children take good care of themselves? (Not really, they are a bit messy.)

艾文想洗澡，但是他只有毛巾，别的用品都不见了。

参考问题和答案：

1 What does Ivan want to do? (He wants to take a shower.)

2 What is Ivan thinking about? (He is thinking about his soap, toothpaste and toothbrush.)

3 What happened to those things? (They are missing and Ivan does not know where they are.)

chuān
穿

加在头、面、颈、手等处。如：戴帽子、戴手套。

dài
戴

qún zi
裙子

jiàn
件

量词"件"用于计量某些个体事物、衣服等。如：一件毛衣。

tiáo
条

量词"条"用于长条形的东西。如：一条路、三条线。

爱莎想穿这条裙子，也想穿那件上衣，还想戴帽子。

参考问题和答案：
1 What is Elsa doing? (She is trying to decide which dress or top to wear.)
2 Do you think Elsa will wear the hat? (Yes, it looks nice.)

第一次独立生活，大家都不知道应该怎么做。

参考问题和答案：
1 What are the children doing? (They are thinking of how their mums helped with their packing.)
2 Do you think the children want to be more independent? (Yes, because they are growing up./No, they are too busy with their schoolwork.)

参考问题和答案：
1 What are the children doing? (They are cooking breakfast.)
2 How do they look? (They look happy.)
3 What do you think Ms Wu is saying? (The breakfast is tasty./As you grow up, you should do more things by yourselves.)

老师说："你们长大了，自己的事应该学习自己做。"

Let's think

1 Recall the activities in the story. Which one did Hao Hao and his friends do? Put a tick or a cross.

2 How well can you do these things? Write the letters.

a 我会做　　b 我不太会做　　c 我不会做

学生做完题目后，老师可以根据图片做调查，看看哪些事情学生做得好，哪些事情不太会做或不会做的，最后鼓励学生多做家务，提高生活自理能力。

New words

1 Learn the new words.

延伸活动：
学生六人一组玩造句接龙游戏。第一个学生用第一张图的生词加上时间造句，
如：爱莎早上七点起床；第二个学生先重复第一个学生的句子，然后用第二张
图的生词再加上时间造句，如：爱莎早上七点起床，她七点半刷牙；以此类推
直到说完第六张图。

起床

刷牙

洗脸、洗澡

想　一条裙子

穿
一件上衣

都戴了帽子

2 Listen to your teacher and point to the correct words above.

听听说说 Listen and say

1 Listen and circle the correct answers.

04 **2** Look at the pictures. Listen to the story an

1 女孩今天八点做什么？

第一题录音稿：
1 我昨天早上八点洗澡，今天早上八点起床，比昨天晚了。

(a) 起床
b 看书
c 洗澡

星期六，我和姐姐不用上学。我们给布朗尼刷牙。

2 女孩穿了什么衣服？

a 雨衣
2 今天很冷，我穿了一条长裤去上学。
(b) 长裤
c 帽子

3 女孩九点做什么？

3 我晚上九点刷牙，我弟弟十点洗脸、洗澡。

a 洗脸
(b) 刷牙
c 洗澡

回到家，我们给布朗尼洗澡，它很高兴。

第二题参考问题和答案：

1 Do Hao Hao and Ling Ling take good care of Brownie? (Yes, they do.)
2 Do you have a pet? How do you take care of it? (I have a dog. I walk him every day./I have some fish. I feed them./I do not have any pets.)

下午，我们去了公园玩，我们一起跑步。

洗了澡，姐姐给布朗尼穿了一件新衣服。小狗真好看！

3 Complete the sentences and role-play with your friend.

a 洗脸　b 洗澡　c 洗手
d 洗衣服　e 刷牙

💬 别玩了，快去 _c_ 。

💬 别玩了，快去 _a_ 。

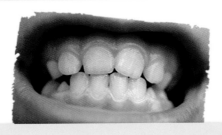

💬 你的牙黄了，快去 _e_ 。

💬 别玩了，快去 _b_ 和 _d_ 。

Task

延伸活动：
学生两人一组，了解对方的日常生活日程，并就组员的情况向全班做报告。

Write about the things you do during a day. Write the numbers and the time. Talk about them with your friend.

> 1 洗脸 2 穿衣服 3 做作业 4 起床 5 放学 6 洗澡
> 7 上床 8 运动 9 玩 10 刷牙 11 上学

活动	星期 _____	👄
	_____ 点 _____ 分	星期一，我六点半起床，七点刷牙、洗澡。我早上八点上学，下午三点十五分放学。我四点半做作业，晚上九点半上床。你呢？
	_____ 点 _____ 分	
	_____ 点 _____ 分	
	_____ 点 _____ 分	
	_____ 点 _____ 分	
	_____ 点 _____ 分	
	_____ 点 _____ 分	
	_____ 点 _____ 分	
	_____ 点 _____ 分	
	_____ 点 _____ 分	

Game

Act out the following actions and ask your friend to say the activity in Chinese.

起床

做运动

刷牙

洗澡

吃早餐

Chant

 Listen and say.

早上六点钟，我们起床、刷牙。
早上六点半，我们洗脸、洗澡。

想一想，今天是晴天还是雨天？
我穿这条长裙，还是那条短裙？
你穿哪件上衣？他穿哪条裤子？

看看天气，穿上衣服，
大家快快乐乐上学去。

学生一边说唱，一边配合歌词做动作；当说到衣物时，指向自己或某同学穿的相应的服装。

生活用语 Daily expressions

都一样。
They are the same.

坏了。

坏了。
It is not working.

15

写一写 Write

1 Trace and write the characters.

丶　丶　氵　氵　汇　泸　泺　泺　洗

洗　洗　洗　洗

一　十　土　丰　丰　走　走　起　起　起
丶　亠　广　广　庐　床　床

起床　起床

2 Write and say.

爱莎说："天气太热了，我要 <u>洗</u> 脸。"

妈妈说："浩浩，八点了，快 <u>起床</u>。"

3 Look at the photos and circle the correct words.

大象喜欢（(洗澡)/洗手）。兔子（rabbit）会（起床/(洗脸)）。小猫（穿衣/(刷牙)）了吗？猴子穿了（帽子/(衣服)）。小狗穿了（(裙子)/裤子）。这些动物真可爱！

拼音输入法 Pinyin input

To type Chinese sentences faster, we can break the sentences into meaningful words instead of individual characters.

1 Type the sentence using two ways. Tick the one which is faster.

早上起床后，大家开始洗脸刷牙。

☐ zao shang qi chuang hou, da jia kai shi xi lian shua ya。

☑ zaoshang qichuang hou, dajia kaishi xilian shuaya。

2 Arrange the words into a meaningful sentence. Write the numbers and type.

xihuan
| 1喜欢 2喜 3嬉 ⬍ |

2

ni
| 1你 2妮 3泥 ⬍ |

1

ma
| 1马 2妈 3吗 ⬍ |

5

xue
| 1学 2雪 3血 ⬍ |

3

zhongwen
| 1中文 2中闻 3中 ⬍ |

4

?

6

提醒学生不要忘记句子中的标点符号。

多元学习 Connections

Cultures

中国小孩日常多穿休闲服，新年时，也会穿传统汉服，即泛指的汉族服装。

1 Do you think Chinese children wear clothes similar to yours? Read what they say.

我们上学穿校服。

我们在草地上玩，我们穿了球鞋。

新年快乐！我们喜欢在新年穿红色的衣服。

In ancient China, the emperor and the princesses wore clothes like this. Now we only wear them to take photos.

天气冷了，我戴了帽子和围巾。

我学打功夫（kungfu），这是我的功夫衣服。

2 Talk about the clothes the children wear for different occasions. 参考表述：

这条裙子是红色和白色的。

男孩穿了黑色的上衣和长裤，女孩穿了白色的长裙子。

她们穿了漂亮的西班牙裙子。

他们穿了美国牛仔衣服，还带了帽子和围巾。

18

提醒学生在折帽子时，对齐角度才会折出又工整又好看的帽子。此外，纸也不要太软太薄。

1 **Fold a paper hat.**

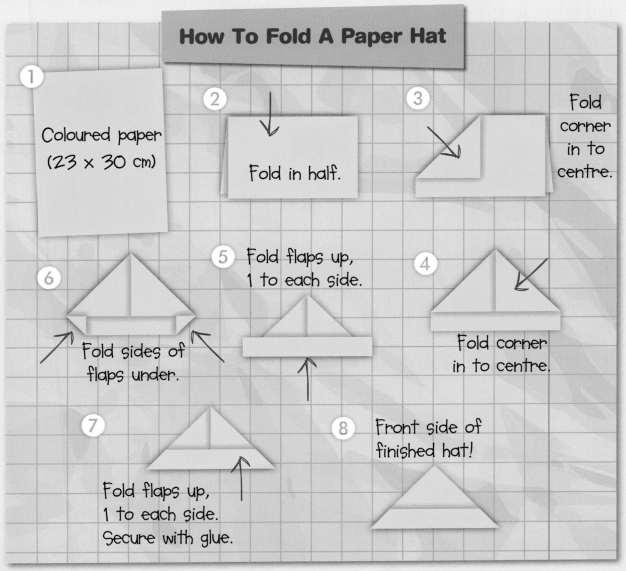

How To Fold A Paper Hat

① Coloured paper (23 x 30 cm)

② Fold in half.

③ Fold corner in to centre.

④ Fold corner in to centre.

⑤ Fold flaps up, 1 to each side.

⑥ Fold sides of flaps under.

⑦ Fold flaps up, 1 to each side. Secure with glue.

⑧ Front side of finished hat!

2 **Play with your friends. Wear the hats and talk about them.**

我们用纸做帽子，真好玩！

我们都戴了帽子，我最喜欢蓝色的。

我想戴这个帽子去跑步。

答题技巧：

选项1至7描写的是人物，a至g是他们的动作或穿的服饰。答题时，先从短句开始配对图片，即a至g，；然后根据图片中人物的性别筛选相应的1至7选项。同时，在填某一选项后，可用斜线画去相应句子前面的数目字或英文字母，以便做下一道填空时，不需重复阅读已用过的句子。

1 Work with your friend. Match the tickets to the pictures and write in the boxes. Then say the following.

1 她想穿	a 洗脸。
2 他用两只手	b 洗澡？
3 他几点起床？	c 刷牙了。
4 她用热水还是冷水	d 你喜欢吗？
5 他这件上衣很好看。	e 他八点起床。
6 穿绿色衣服的男孩	f 和大大的帽子。
7 她戴了长长的围巾	g 那条白色的裙子。

起 床

3e 6c 2a 4b

7f 5d 1g

想

20

评核方法：
学生两人一组，互相考察评价表内单词和句子的听说读写。交际沟通部分由老师朗读要求，
学生再互相对话。如果达到了某项技能要求，则用色笔将星星或小辣椒涂色。

2 Work with your friend. Colour the stars and the chillies.

Words	说	读	写
起床	☆	☆	☆
洗脸	☆	☆	🌶
刷牙	☆	☆	🌶
洗澡	☆	☆	🌶
想	☆	☆	☆
穿	☆	☆	🌶
上衣	☆	☆	🌶
了	☆	☆	🌶
都	☆	🌶	🌶
戴	☆	🌶	🌶

Words and sentences	说	读	写
条	☆	🌶	🌶
件	☆	🌶	🌶
裙子	☆	🌶	🌶
别的用品都不见了。	☆	🌶	🌶
你们长大了。	☆	🌶	🌶

Talk about daily routine	☆

3 What does your teacher say?

评核建议：
根据学生课堂表现，分别给予"太棒了！
(Excellent!)"、"不错！(Good!)"或"继续努力！
(Work harder!)"的评价，再让学生圈出左侧对
应的表情，以记录自己的学习情况。

My teacher says...

分享 Sharing

Words I remember

起床	qǐ chuáng	to get up
洗脸	xǐ liǎn	to wash one's face
刷牙	shuā yá	to brush one's teeth
洗澡	xǐ zǎo	to shower, to bath
想	xiǎng	to want to, to think
穿	chuān	to wear
上衣	shàng yī	tops
了	le	(to indicate a change of state or the completion of an action)
都	dōu	both, all
戴	dài	to wear on top
条	tiáo	(measure word for dresses, skirts, pants, etc.)
件	jiàn	(measure word for tops)
裙子	qún zi	dress, skirt

延伸活动：

1 学生用手遮盖英文，读中文单词，并思考单词意思；

2 学生用手遮盖中文单词，看着英文说出对应的中文单词；

3 学生三人一组，尽量运用中文单词分角色复述故事。

Other words

次	cì	(measure word for frequency)
露营	lù yíng	to go camping
高兴	gāo xìng	happy
只有	zhǐ yǒu	only
后	hòu	afterwards
毛巾	máo jīn	towel
用品	yòng pǐn	articles for use
独立	dú lì	on one's own
应该	yīng gāi	ought to, must
老师	lǎo shī	teacher
长大	zhǎng dà	to grow up
自己	zì jǐ	oneself
事	shì	thing
学习	xué xí	to learn

OXFORD
UNIVERSITY PRESS

Oxford University Press is a department of the University of Oxford.
It furthers the University's objective of excellence in research, scholarship,
and education by publishing worldwide. Oxford is a registered trade mark of
Oxford University Press in the UK and in certain other countries

Published in Hong Kong by
Oxford University Press (China) Limited
39th Floor, One Kowloon, 1 Wang Yuen Street, Kowloon Bay,
Hong Kong

Illustrated by Anne Lee, Emily Chan, KY Chan and Wildman

Photographs for reproduction permitted by Dreamstime.com

China National Publications Import & Export (Group) Corporation is an authorized distributor of
Oxford Elementary Chinese.

Please contact content@cnpiec.com.cn or 86-10-65856782

ISBN: 978-0-19-082256-9

10 9 8 7 6 5 4 3 2

Teacher's Edition
ISBN: 978-0-19-082268-2

10 9 8 7 6 5 4 3 2